for YOU
my ZIGGY FRIeND!

ZiGGYS
OF THE WORLD
UNiTE!

BY Tom Wilson

Sheed Andrews and McMeel, Inc.
Subsidiary of Universal Press Syndicate
Kansas City

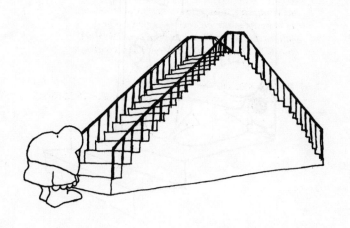

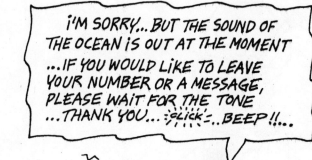

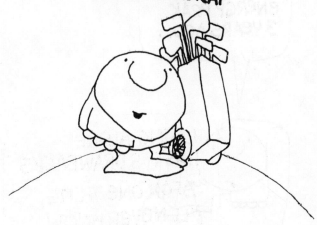

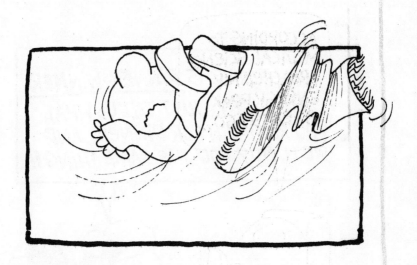

...SOMEDAYS i FeeL ABOUT AS USELESS AS A DUST JACKET ON A DIRTY BOOK...

..FAMOUS PEOPLE WEAR SUN GLASSES SO PEOPLE WON'T KNOW WHO THEY ARE

...i WEAR THEM SO PEOPLE WON'T KNOW WHO i'M NOT !!

...i CAN TAKE THE PUBLISHERS REJECTING MY POEMS...

BUT LATELY THE REJECTS HAVE BEEN COMING BY SPECIAL DELIVERY !!

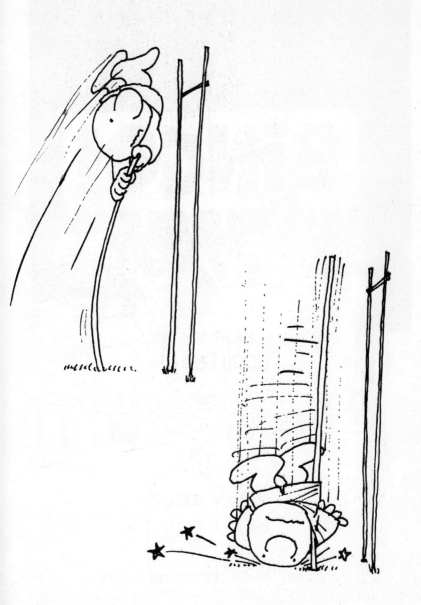

click

...EVEN MY MARGARINE ISN'T
SPEAKING TO ME !!

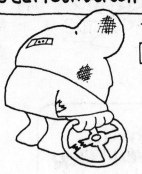

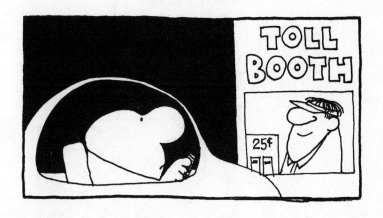

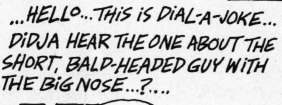

SOMEONE TOLD
ME THAT IF i PUT
A PENNY IN MY
SHOE iT WOULD
BRING ME GOOD
LUCK ...
SO i TRIED iT..

...GOT THE BIGGEST
BLISTER YOU EVER
SAW !!

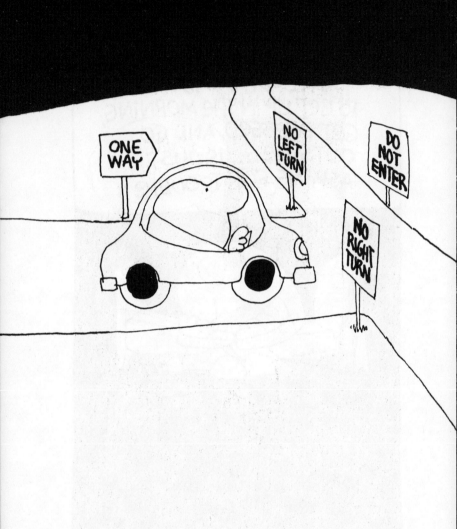

COSMETIC
SURGEON

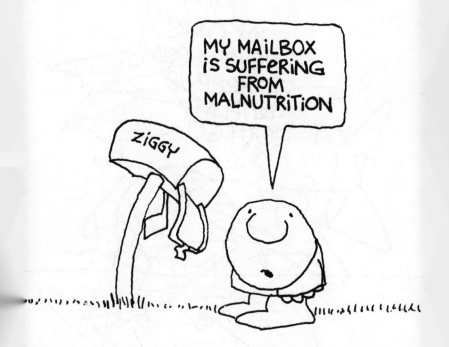

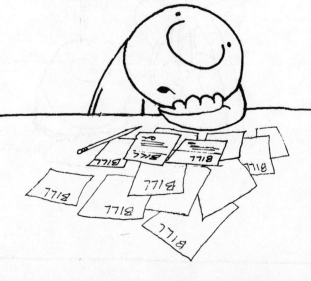

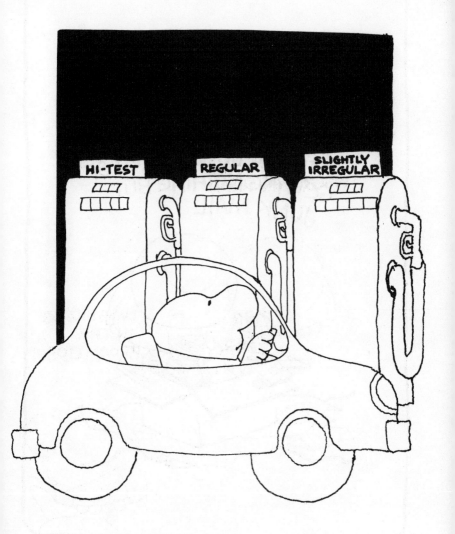

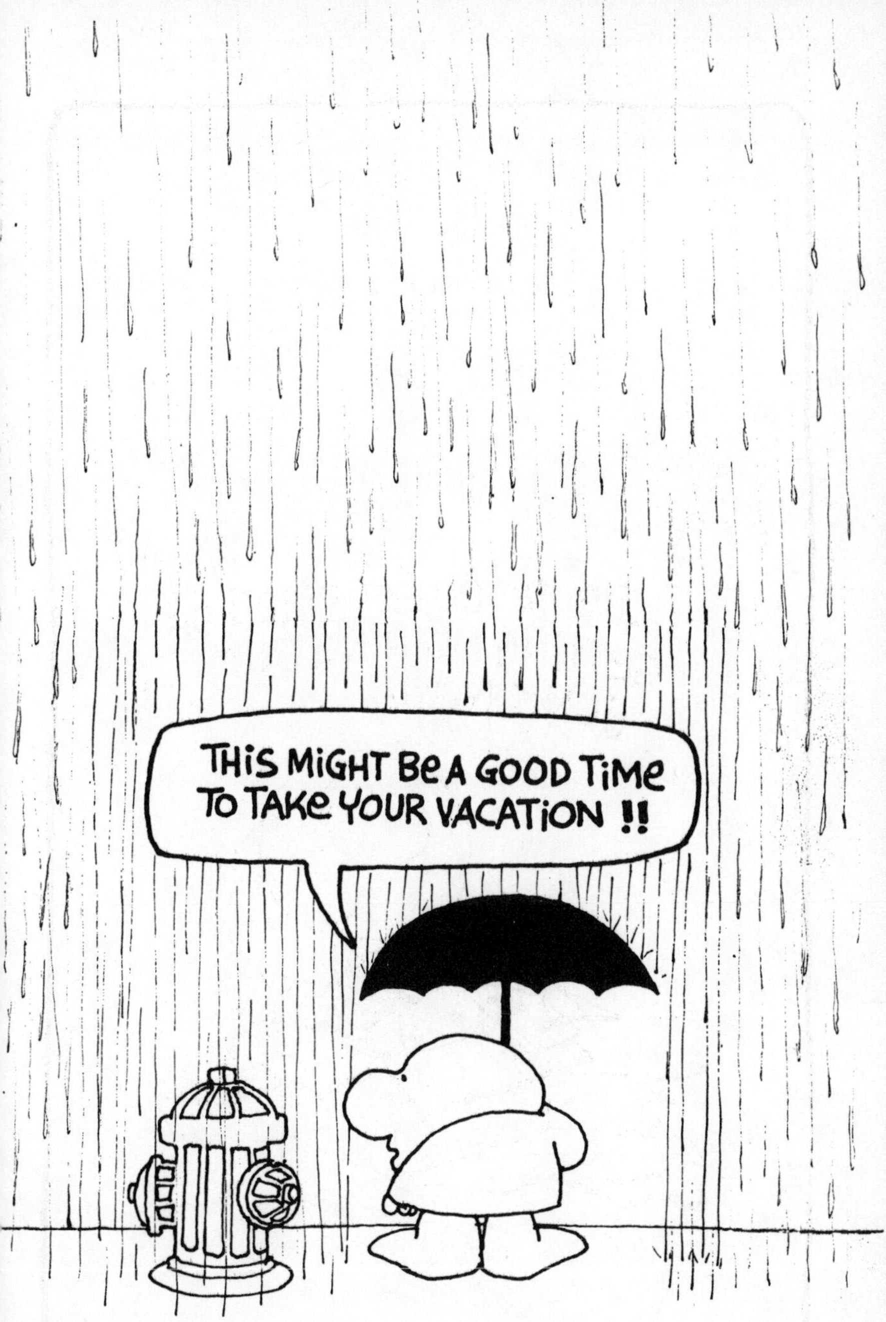
THIS MIGHT BE A GOOD TIME TO TAKE YOUR VACATION !!